This Belongs To:

_____

_____

Our

Q & A

A Day

3-Year Journal for Couples

January

1

How do you envision yourself this new year?

20____

20____

20____

2

What good you received last year in the form of
hope, faith, inspiration or in many other ways?

20____

20____

20____

January

3

What are your highest passions that you haven't yet begun acting on?

20____ _____

_____

_____

_____

_____

_____

20____ _____

_____

_____

_____

_____

_____

20____ _____

_____

_____

_____

_____

_____

4

If you could spend one day in someone else's shoes,
who would it be and why?

20____ _____

_____

_____

_____

20____ _____

_____

_____

_____

20____ _____

_____

_____

_____

5

How do you respond to someone who has different
perspectives, values, or beliefs?

20_____ _____

_____

_____

_____

_____

20_____ _____

_____

_____

_____

_____

20_____ _____

_____

_____

_____

_____

6

What do you value and appreciate in relationship?

20___

20___

20___

January

7

How do you plan to nurture yourself physically
mentally spiritually this year?

20____ _____

_____

_____

_____

_____

20____ _____

_____

_____

_____

_____

20____ _____

_____

_____

_____

_____

8

What does loving someone while keeping healthy boundaries look like?

20____

20____

20____

January

9

Embrace your partner for at least one minute and
write down your feelings

20____ _____

_____

_____

_____

20____ _____

_____

_____

_____

20____ _____

_____

_____

_____

10

Leave messages to yourself when you were 5-12
years old

20_____ _____

_____

_____

_____

_____

20_____ _____

_____

_____

_____

_____

20_____ _____

_____

_____

_____

_____

January

11

What does love mean to you?

20_____ _____

_____

_____

_____

_____

20_____ _____

_____

_____

_____

_____

20_____ _____

_____

_____

_____

_____

12

What is your mind focused on recently and why?

20_____

20_____

20_____

January

13

What keeps you going day to day?

20____ _____

_____

_____

_____

_____

20____ _____

_____

_____

_____

_____

20____ _____

_____

_____

_____

_____

14

What are the best things about your relationship?

20____

20____

20____

January

15

What did you learn about marriage from your parents?

20_____ _____

_____

_____

_____

_____

20_____ _____

_____

_____

_____

_____

20_____ _____

_____

_____

_____

_____

16

Based on your experiences, what advice would you
give to people who are dating?

20_____

_____

20_____

_____

20_____

_____

January

17

Is there a memory you have of your partner that
always makes you laugh?

20_____ _____

_____

_____

_____

_____

20_____ _____

_____

_____

_____

_____

20_____ _____

_____

_____

_____

_____

18

Recommend 5 books that everyone should read

20____

_____

_____

_____

_____

20____

_____

_____

_____

_____

20____

_____

_____

_____

_____

19

How do you cultivate the inner work on self-respect
and self-worth?

20_____ _____

20_____ _____

20_____ _____

20

How is your relationship with yourself?

20_____ _____

_____

_____

_____

20_____ _____

_____

_____

_____

20_____ _____

_____

_____

_____

January

21

How do you respond to situations that force you to get out of your comfort zone?

20____ _____

20____ _____

20____ _____

22

What will make your relationship stronger?

20_____ _____

_____

_____

_____

20_____ _____

_____

_____

_____

20_____ _____

_____

_____

_____

January

23

What challenges are your grateful for?

20_____

_____

_____

_____

_____

20_____

_____

_____

_____

_____

20_____

_____

_____

_____

_____

24

Write a love note to yourself

20____

20____

20____

January

25

How do you define yourself?

20_____ _____

20_____ _____

20_____ _____

26

A few of your favorite things

20____

20____

20____

January

27

If tomorrow is the end of the earth, what would your ideal last day be like?

20____ _____

_____

_____

_____

_____

20____ _____

_____

_____

_____

_____

20____ _____

_____

_____

_____

_____

28

Your first impression or earliest memories on
meeting your partner

20____ _____

_____

_____

_____

20____ _____

_____

_____

_____

20____ _____

_____

_____

_____

January

29

What are you grateful for today?

20_____ _____

20_____ _____

20_____ _____

30

What do you love about being you, make a list

20_____ _____

_____

_____

_____

_____

20_____ _____

_____

_____

_____

_____

20_____ _____

_____

_____

_____

_____

January

31

A love note to your partner

20_____ _____

20_____ _____

20_____ _____

1

Imagine you are in your 90s. What stories would you
like to tell

20_____

20_____

20_____

February

2

What are you the most excited for this year?

20_____

_____

20_____

_____

20_____

_____

3

What hobby would you like to take up together?

20____

_____

_____

_____

_____

20____

_____

_____

_____

_____

20____

_____

_____

_____

_____

February

4

What's the best surprise you have ever received?

20___ _____

_____

_____

_____

20___ _____

_____

_____

_____

20___ _____

_____

_____

_____

5

How comfortable are you to feel vulnerable?

20___ _____

_____

_____

_____

_____

20___ _____

_____

_____

_____

_____

20___ _____

_____

_____

_____

_____

February

6

If you had 6 months to live, what would be the most important things for you?

20_____ _____

_____

_____

_____

_____

20_____ _____

_____

_____

_____

_____

20_____ _____

_____

_____

_____

_____

7

How do you respond when someone judges you or makes fun of you?

20____

_____

_____

_____

_____

20____

_____

_____

_____

_____

20____

_____

_____

_____

_____

February

8

What things you do that inspire, evolve and lift you higher?

20_____ _____

_____

_____

_____

20_____ _____

_____

_____

_____

20_____ _____

_____

_____

_____

9

Which activities make you lose track of time?

20_____ _____

20_____ _____

20_____ _____

10

What areas in life that you take yourself too seriously?

20_____ _____

_____

_____

_____

_____

20_____ _____

_____

_____

_____

_____

20_____ _____

_____

_____

_____

_____

11

List 5 things you love about yourself today?

20_____ _____

_____

_____

_____

_____

20_____ _____

_____

_____

_____

20_____ _____

_____

_____

_____

February

12

What words or beliefs do you want to live your life
by?

20_____ _____

_____

_____

_____

20_____ _____

_____

_____

_____

_____

20_____ _____

_____

_____

_____

13

List 5 things you adore about your partner

20_____ _____

_____

_____

_____

_____

_____

20_____ _____

_____

_____

_____

_____

20_____ _____

_____

_____

_____

_____

February

14

Top 3 "I loved you" moments

20____ _____

_____

_____

_____

_____

20____ _____

_____

_____

_____

_____

20____ _____

_____

_____

_____

_____

15

If you could become the number one expert in one
niche field, what would it be?

20____ _____

_____

_____

_____

_____

_____

20____ _____

_____

_____

_____

_____

_____

20____ _____

_____

_____

_____

_____

February

16

Who is your favorite author and why?

20_____ _____

_____

_____

_____

_____

20_____ _____

_____

_____

_____

_____

20_____ _____

_____

_____

_____

_____

17

Where do you want to live when you retire and why?

20_____

20_____

20_____

February

18

What are your goals this year?

20_____ _____

_____

_____

_____

_____

20_____ _____

_____

_____

_____

_____

20_____ _____

_____

_____

_____

_____

19

What things you said to your partner were spoken with love?

20_____

_____

20_____

_____

20_____

_____

February

20

What kinds of things put smile on your face?

20_____ _____

20_____ _____

20_____ _____

21

If you could have dinner with 3 people(dead or alive), who would they be and why?

20_____

_____

_____

_____

_____

20_____

_____

_____

_____

_____

20_____

_____

_____

_____

_____

February

22

Describe how you feel about yourself in 3 or more adjective

20_____ _____

20_____ _____

20_____ _____

23

Your favorite childhood memory and what made it
so special to you?

20_____

_____

20_____

_____

20_____

_____

February

24

If you had to choose one word to focus on this year,
it would be... why?

20___

20___

20___

25

List self-empowering and loving affirmations

20____ _____

20____ _____

20____ _____

February

26

Observe your talks for one day- Is it true, is it kind, is it necessary?

20_____

20_____

20_____

27

Experience one day without complaining or arguing,
write how you feel

20____ _____

_____

_____

_____

_____

20____ _____

_____

_____

_____

_____

20____ _____

_____

_____

_____

_____

February

28

Hold hands while looking into each other's eyes at
least one minutes, write your feelings

20_____ _____

20_____ _____

20_____ _____

1

What gives meaning to your life?

20___

20___

20___

March

2

What qualities does your partner possess that made
you think they are special?

20____ _____

_____

_____

_____

_____

20____ _____

_____

_____

_____

_____

20____ _____

_____

_____

_____

_____

3

What does self-love mean to you?

20____

20____

20____

March

4

What's the most scared you ever felt, as a child?

20_____ _____

20_____ _____

20_____ _____

5

Do you believe in God, describe the God you believe

20_____ _____

20_____

20_____

6

What's your favorite memory with your siblings?

20____

_____

20____

_____

20____

_____

7

In what areas is it hardest to be "totally" open and honest with your partner?

20____

_____

_____

_____

_____

20____

_____

_____

_____

_____

20____

_____

_____

_____

_____

March

8

How well are you serving each other?

20_____ _____

20_____ _____

20_____ _____

9

If a crystal ball could tell you the truth about yourself,
what would you want to know?

20____ _____

_____

_____

_____

_____

20____ _____

_____

_____

_____

_____

20____ _____

_____

_____

_____

_____

March

10

How do you envision your future?

20____ _____

_____

_____

_____

_____

20____ _____

_____

_____

_____

_____

20____ _____

_____

_____

_____

_____

11

How do you express love, do people easily recognize
your "love language"?

20_____

20_____

20_____

March

12

What would you do if you weren't so afraid of failing?

20____ _____

_____

_____

_____

_____

20____ _____

_____

_____

_____

_____

20____ _____

_____

_____

_____

_____

13

Your favorite inspirational quote that makes you
think of your partner and why?

20_____

20_____

20_____

March

14

Where do you feel safe, loved and grateful for?

20_____

20_____

20_____

15

What books will you like to read, why?

20_____

20_____

20_____

March

16

How can you be a better listener?

20____ _____

20____ _____

20____ _____

17

Your definition on abundance?

20____

20____

20____

March

18

What are 2 life lessons you have learned so far?

20_____

20_____

20_____

19

This year I will embrace… I will focus on…

20___

20___

20___

March

20

Uplifting conversations you have had

20_____ _____

_____

_____

_____

_____

20_____ _____

_____

_____

_____

_____

20_____ _____

_____

_____

_____

_____

21

What do you love about your life right now? Why do you love it?

20_____

_____

_____

_____

_____

20_____

_____

_____

_____

_____

20_____

_____

_____

_____

_____

March

22

Share a childhood memory you've never shared
before

20____ _____

_____

_____

_____

20____ _____

_____

_____

_____

_____

20____ _____

_____

_____

_____

_____

23

What desires do you have that haven't been discussed?

20_____

20_____

20_____

March

24

If you could donate a million dollars to a cause, what would it be? Why?

20____ _____

_____

_____

_____

_____

20____ _____

_____

_____

_____

_____

20____ _____

_____

_____

_____

_____

25

Write a piece of real mail to someone who would it
be and why?

20_____ _____

20_____ _____

20_____ _____

March

26

What legacy would you like to leave?

20_____

20_____

20_____

27

How mindful are you? How often do you live in the present moment of now?

20_____

20_____

20_____

March

28

A love poem to your partner

20_____

20_____

20_____

29

"I open to receive love and to recognize love in all of its forms" how do you feel about this affirmation?

20_____

20_____

20_____

March

30

Ask your inner child what it's frightened of. As an adult, write comforting words to that child

20____ _____

_____

_____

_____

20____ _____

_____

_____

_____

20____ _____

_____

_____

_____

31

Last year was a year of…This year will be a year of…

20____

20____

20____

April

1

How/what would you like to create a new-self from habitual-self who thinks, feels, acts differently?

20____ _____

_____

_____

_____

_____

20____ _____

_____

_____

_____

_____

20____ _____

_____

_____

_____

_____

2

How do you feel about gray hair and wrinkle?

20____

20____

20____

April

3

How do you respond to "bad" or inconvenient news?

20____

20____

20____

4

I am blessed because…

20___ _____

_____

_____

_____

_____

20___ _____

_____

_____

_____

_____

20___ _____

_____

_____

_____

_____

April

5

What is something you need to start saying Yes or No to?

20_____ _____

20_____ _____

20_____ _____

6

What is your favorite memory with your partner recently?

20_____

_____

20_____

_____

20_____

_____

April

7

What have your partner helped you accept about
yourself, how

20_____

20_____

20_____

8

Outdated beliefs, thoughts, feelings that do not
serve you and you like to let them go?

20_____

_____

_____

_____

_____

20_____

_____

_____

_____

_____

20_____

_____

_____

_____

_____

April

9

What subjects are you interested in, like to know
more and research on?

20_____ _____

20_____ _____

20_____ _____

10

"If ...I will be happy" What is unconditional
happiness meant to you?

20_____

20_____

20_____

April

11

Write an encouraging note to your previous self who
was experiencing great pain or heart-ache

20____ _____

_____

_____

_____

20____ _____

_____

_____

_____

20____ _____

_____

_____

_____

12

Which friend/family member are you grateful for?

20＿＿＿ ＿＿＿＿＿＿＿＿＿＿＿＿＿＿＿＿＿＿＿＿

20＿＿＿ ＿＿＿＿＿＿＿＿＿＿＿＿＿＿＿＿＿＿＿＿

20＿＿＿ ＿＿＿＿＿＿＿＿＿＿＿＿＿＿＿＿＿＿＿＿

April

13

If you had to make a marital bucket list what would
be on it?

20_____

20_____

20_____

14

Your painful experiences that serve your growth and
reshape your perspective

20_____

20_____

20_____

April

15

What do you like to learn this year?

20___ _____

_____

_____

_____

_____

20___ _____

_____

_____

_____

_____

20___ _____

_____

_____

_____

_____

16

How to worry less and smile more?

20_____

20_____

20_____

April

17

List appreciation to your body

20___ _____

_____

_____

_____

_____

20___ _____

_____

_____

_____

_____

20___ _____

_____

_____

_____

_____

18

Write a love note and hide it somewhere you know it
will be found

20____

_____

20____

_____

20____

_____

April

19

What does imperfection mean to you? How can you
learn to embrace imperfection in your life?

20____

20____

20____

20

What's your favorite personality trait of your own
and why?

20_____

_____

20_____

_____

20_____

_____

April

21

The most important qualities you see in a friend?

20___

_____

_____

_____

_____

20___

_____

_____

_____

_____

20___

_____

_____

_____

_____

22

Imagine one morning you wake up and you found
yourself in the body of…, you would…?

20____

20____

20____

April

23

A favorite song lyric, why it is your favorite?

20____ _____

20____ _____

20____ _____

24

If you could ask questions to some 90 years old, what would you ask?

20_____

_____

_____

_____

_____

20_____

_____

_____

_____

_____

20_____

_____

_____

_____

_____

April

25

How do you treat yourself emotionally?

20___ _____

20___ _____

20___ _____

26

Did you make someone smile recently, how or why?

20___

20___

20___

April

27

What food cooked by your partner that you are grateful for?

20_____

20_____

20_____

28

How would you describe yourself in a loving way to a stranger?

20____

20____

20____

April

29

When did you know your partner was the one for you, how?

20_____

20_____

20_____

30

What is your biggest fear/joy in life? why?

20_____

_____

20_____

_____

20_____

_____

May

1

Who do you like to spend more time with and why?

20____ _____

_____

_____

_____

_____

20____ _____

_____

_____

_____

_____

20____ _____

_____

_____

_____

_____

2

What you have missed the most when you and your
partner have been apart?

20_____ _____

_____

_____

_____

20_____ _____

_____

_____

_____

20_____ _____

_____

_____

_____

May

3

What are your favorite books and why?

20_____

20_____

20_____

4

If you could give your younger self some advices,
what would they be?

20_____

20_____

20_____

May

5

What are your favorite moments with your partner?

20_____

20_____

20_____

6

" We suffer more often in imagination than in reality-
Seneca" your reflection on this quo?

20_____ _____

_____

_____

_____

_____

20_____ _____

_____

_____

_____

_____

20_____ _____

_____

_____

_____

_____

May

7

Set intention and do something nice for your partner
today

20____ _____

20____ _____

20____ _____

8

Describe your life theme in few words

20___

20___

20___

May

9

What was the most beautiful view you have ever experienced?

20_____ _____

_____

_____

_____

20_____ _____

_____

_____

_____

20_____ _____

_____

_____

_____

10

How do you define "success"

20_____

20_____

20_____

May

11

What do you do to keep the spark alive in your
relationship?

20_____

20_____

20_____

12

Free writing: Love is…, freedom is…, beauty is….

20_____

20_____

20_____

May

13

What's your favorite memory with your mom?

20_____

20_____

20_____

14

Describe your favorite pets or animals

20____

20____

20____

May

15

If you were a TV show producer, what kind of show
would you produce and why?

20____ _____

_____

_____

_____

_____

20____ _____

_____

_____

_____

_____

20____ _____

_____

_____

_____

_____

16

What's the worst job you have ever had and what do you learn about yourself?

20_____

_____

_____

_____

_____

_____

20_____

_____

_____

_____

_____

_____

20_____

_____

_____

_____

_____

_____

May

17

Describe your dream vacation

20____

20____

20____

18

What is your favorite family tradition?

20____

20____

20____

May

19

Name 3 things you and your partner have in common

20_____ _____

_____
_____
_____
_____
_____

20_____ _____

_____
_____
_____
_____
_____

20_____ _____

_____
_____
_____
_____

20

How your partner makes you feel good about yourself?

20____

20____

20____

May

21

When are the times you can spend time alone for the
peace of solitude and silence?

20_____ _____

_____

_____

_____

_____

20_____ _____

_____

_____

_____

_____

20_____ _____

_____

_____

_____

_____

22

What thoughts strengthen you?

20____

20____

20____

May

23

An embarrassing moment in your life?

20_____ _____
_____
_____
_____
_____
_____

20_____ _____
_____
_____
_____
_____
_____

20_____ _____
_____
_____
_____
_____

24

What did your partner do make your feel loved?

20_____

_____

20_____

_____

20_____

_____

May

25

What about your body you are grateful for?

20_____ _____

_____

_____

_____

_____

20_____ _____

_____

_____

_____

_____

20_____ _____

_____

_____

_____

_____

26

What need to work on the most in your relationship?

20_____ _____

_____

_____

_____

_____

20_____ _____

_____

_____

_____

_____

20_____ _____

_____

_____

_____

_____

May

27

When was last time you cry and why?

20____ _____
_____
_____
_____
_____

20____ _____
_____
_____
_____
_____

20____ _____
_____
_____
_____
_____

28

The songs in your life soundtrack?

20_____

20_____

20_____

May

29

Compliments you have received

20_____ _____
_____
_____
_____
_____

20_____ _____
_____
_____
_____
_____

20_____ _____
_____
_____
_____
_____

30

Could you love whatever arise for you to experience
even those you label "bad", why or why not?

20____

20____

20____

May

31

A list of things that give you energy

20_____ _____

_____

_____

_____

_____

20_____ _____

_____

_____

_____

_____

20_____ _____

_____

_____

_____

_____

1

"Know thyself" How much/deep do you know about yourself?

20_____

20_____

20_____

June

2

Happiness is a state of mind. What is your happiness state?

20_____ _____

_____

_____

_____

_____

20_____ _____

_____

_____

_____

_____

20_____ _____

_____

_____

_____

_____

3

If you were a school teacher of 1st graders, what
would you teach your students? and why

20_____

20_____

20_____

June

4

Any project/plan you have been putting off, why?

20_____ _____

_____

_____

_____

_____

20_____ _____

_____

_____

_____

_____

20_____ _____

_____

_____

_____

_____

5

What are 3 positive thoughts you like to have?

20_____ _____

_____

_____

_____

_____

20_____ _____

_____

_____

_____

_____

20_____ _____

_____

_____

_____

_____

June

6

If your life is a novel, what would the title and
subtitle be and why?

20_____

20_____

20_____

7

How fulfilling is your day today?

20_____

20_____

20_____

June

8

Express gratitude to 2 people who no longer with you

20_____ _____

20_____ _____

20_____ _____

9

What makes you feel powerful and lit up?

20_____

20_____

20_____

June

10

What fun/crazy things would you like to try?

20____

_____

20____

_____

20____

_____

11

When you wake up in the morning, how do you most want to feel?

20_____

20_____

20_____

June

12

Describe various dream dates – a romantic date, fun
date, casual date...

20_____ _____

_____

_____

_____

_____

20_____ _____

_____

_____

_____

_____

20_____ _____

_____

_____

_____

_____

13

What are the greatest strength in your relationship?

20____ _____

_____

_____

_____

_____

_____

20____ _____

_____

_____

_____

_____

20____ _____

_____

_____

_____

_____

June

14

Has your parent's relationship life effected your view
of love, how?

20_____ _____

_____

_____

_____

_____

20_____ _____

_____

_____

_____

_____

20_____ _____

_____

_____

_____

_____

15

What quality/energy you like to embody?

20____

_____

_____

_____

_____

_____

20____

_____

_____

_____

_____

_____

20____

_____

_____

_____

_____

_____

June

16

What food/drinks you are grateful for, why?

20____

20____

20____

17

What's your favorite memory with your dad?

20____

20____

20____

June

18

What is something your partner does that you think
is sexy?

20____ _____

20____ _____

20____ _____

19

Where in your life do you need to slow down or
speed up?

20_____

20_____

20_____

June

20

What's one choice you can make right now that your
future self will thank you?

20_____

20_____

20_____

21

What labels, negative and positive, do you assign yourself?

20____

20____

20____

June

22

Things that bring you joy that money can't buy?

20____ _____

_____

_____

_____

_____

20____ _____

_____

_____

_____

_____

20____ _____

_____

_____

_____

_____

23

Something you have been assuming control over
and need to release to the orchestration of the
Universe is..?

20____

_____

_____

_____

_____

_____

20____

_____

_____

_____

_____

_____

20____

_____

_____

_____

_____

June

24

Look into the eyes of your partner for one minute
and write down how you feel

20____ _____

_____

_____

_____

_____

20____ _____

_____

_____

_____

_____

20____ _____

_____

_____

_____

_____

25

Reflect on a recent inspiring quote and what it
means in your life

20_____

20_____

20_____

June

26

Traits you think you've inherited from your parents and what traits your partner has inherited from theirs?

20_____ _____

_____

_____

_____

_____

20_____ _____

_____

_____

_____

_____

20_____ _____

_____

_____

_____

_____

27

A book you re-read a lot and why?

20____

_____

20____

_____

20____

_____

28

How do you respond to other people's mistakes or unpleasant behavior?

20____ _____

20____ _____

20____ _____

29

One thing you learned about yourself recently?

20___

20___

20___

June

30

Who is your "cheerleader" and who do you cheer up?

20____

20____

20____

1

List your favorite activities together with your partner

20___ _____

_____

_____

_____

20___ _____

_____

_____

_____

20___ _____

_____

_____

_____

2

What would you Not do for 1 million dollars?

20_____ _____

_____

_____

_____

20_____ _____

_____

_____

_____

20_____ _____

_____

_____

_____

3

What is society doing now that in 20 years will be unbelievable?

20_____ _____

_____

_____

_____

20_____ _____

_____

_____

_____

20_____ _____

_____

_____

_____

July

4

What have you done to deepen your love?

20____

20____

20____

5

What one question can you ask someone to find out
the most about them and why?

20____

20____

20____

6

What stories from your life will you tell your children
about (assuming you have children)?

20____ _____

_____

_____

_____

_____

20____ _____

_____

_____

_____

_____

20____ _____

_____

_____

_____

_____

7

What's the most unusual and fun experience you 've had?

20_____ _____

_____

_____

_____

_____

20_____ _____

_____

_____

_____

_____

20_____ _____

_____

_____

_____

_____

July

8

How do you deal with the emotion- anger?

20____ _____

20____ _____

20____ _____

9

Do you see yourself as an optimist, pessimist or
realist, and why?

20_____

20_____

20_____

July

10

How was your upbringing impacted you as a person?

20____ _____

_____

_____

_____

_____

20____ _____

_____

_____

_____

_____

20____ _____

_____

_____

_____

_____

11

Something your partner don't know about you and you like your partner to know?

20_____ _____

_____

_____

_____

_____

20_____ _____

_____

_____

_____

_____

20_____ _____

_____

_____

_____

_____

July

12

What are your current hubbies and new hubbies you like to develop?

20____ _____

20____ _____

20____ _____

13

If you were stuck on a deserted island and you could
only bring one item and one book, what would they
be and why?

20____ _____

_____

_____

_____

_____

20____ _____

_____

_____

_____

_____

20____ _____

_____

_____

_____

_____

July

14

What are limiting beliefs you have about yourself
that you like to let go?

20_____

_____

_____

_____

_____

_____

20_____

_____

_____

_____

_____

_____

20_____

_____

_____

_____

_____

_____

15

How do you handle "change" in life?

20____

20____

20____

16

What would you be, say or do to a person who is
dying and dear to your heart?

20____ _____
_____
_____
_____
_____

20____ _____
_____
_____
_____
_____

20____ _____
_____
_____
_____
_____

17

What do you enjoy in alone time?

20_____

20_____

20_____

July

18

Ask yourself a question and answer it

20____

20____

20____

19

A love note to your partner

20_____ _____

20_____ _____

20_____ _____

20

How easy it is for you to love yourself unconditionally
based on who you are not what you do?

20_____

20_____

20_____

21

What has shaken the core of your being, why?

20____

20____

20____

July

22

What makes your partner different from everyone else?

20_____ _____

20_____ _____

20_____ _____

23

What would your younger self be proud of you today?

20____

_____

_____

_____

_____

20____

_____

_____

_____

_____

20____

_____

_____

_____

_____

July

24

What themes in life you like to explore?

20____ _____
_____
_____
_____
_____

20____ _____
_____
_____
_____
_____

20____ _____
_____
_____
_____
_____

25

Times or things in your relationship that were
challenging and then how you got over them or
learned from them?

20_____

20_____

20_____

26

What beliefs are holding you back from being who you truly are?

20_____ _____

_____

_____

_____

20_____ _____

_____

_____

_____

20_____ _____

_____

_____

_____

27

How can you show yourself more unconditional
love?

20_____

20_____

20_____

28

If you had to teach something, what would you like to teach?

20____

20____

20____

29

Simple things in life you appreciate

20_____

20_____

20_____

July

30

How do you deal with being misperceived or
misunderstood?

20____

20____

20____

31

What are you passionate about?

20_____

20_____

20_____

August

1

How much do you prioritize spending time and
energy on yourself and on your passion?

20____ _____

_____

_____

_____

_____

20____ _____

_____

_____

_____

_____

20____ _____

_____

_____

_____

_____

2

What would you say to someone who is undergoing depression?

20____

20____

20____

August

3

Times when you deep-belly laughed together?

20_____

20_____

20_____

4

I can take better care of my emotional health by…

20_____ _____

20_____ _____

20_____ _____

August

5

When did your heart say yes and your head say no,
or vice versa?

20_____ _____

_____

_____

_____

_____

20_____ _____

_____

_____

_____

_____

20_____ _____

_____

_____

_____

_____

6

What experiences you have had with your partner
that helps you to know more about yourself?

20____

20____

20____

August

7

I give myself permission slip to…

20____ _____

_____

_____

_____

_____

20____ _____

_____

_____

_____

_____

20____ _____

_____

_____

_____

_____

8

Have you ever based your worth on the approval of
others, how and why?

20_____ _____

_____

_____

_____

_____

20_____ _____

_____

_____

_____

_____

20_____ _____

_____

_____

_____

_____

August

9

List your random acts of kindness

20_____ _____

_____

_____

_____

_____

20_____ _____

_____

_____

_____

_____

20_____ _____

_____

_____

_____

_____

10

If life stop today, what would you regret not doing?

20____ _____

_____

_____

_____

_____

20____ _____

_____

_____

_____

_____

20____ _____

_____

_____

_____

_____

August

11

Write a love letter to your inner child who likes to
heal and loved

20_____ _____
_____
_____
_____
_____

20_____ _____
_____
_____
_____
_____

20_____ _____
_____
_____
_____
_____

12

Describe your partner in three words

20___

20___

20___

August

13

What do you judge people for most often?

20____ _____

_____

_____

_____

20____ _____

_____

_____

_____

20____ _____

_____

_____

_____

14

Who are some people you only met once but they
left a big impression on you and why?

20____

20____

20____

August

15

What is the highest pressure situation you have experienced and how did you handle it?

20_____ _____

_____

_____

_____

_____

20_____ _____

_____

_____

_____

_____

20_____ _____

_____

_____

_____

_____

16

I love spending time with you and sometimes I need
alone time to…

20____ _____

_____

_____

_____

20____ _____

_____

_____

_____

20____ _____

_____

_____

_____

August

17

What is it about your partner that will put a smile on your face?

20____ _____

_____

_____

_____

_____

20____ _____

_____

_____

_____

_____

20____ _____

_____

_____

_____

_____

18

What's the best thing about being male/female?

20_____

20_____

20_____

August

19

What would you say to a person who just lost a loved one?

20_____

20_____

20_____

20

If you had to choose one cause to dedicate your life
to, what would that cause be?

20_____

20_____

20_____

August

21

What do you spend most of your time doing?

20____

20____

20____

22

Describe yourself in three words?

20_____

20_____

20_____

August

23

What is one thing you want to do different from your parents?

20____ _____

_____

_____

_____

20____ _____

_____

_____

_____

20____ _____

_____

_____

_____

24

Ask your inner child, is there any unresolved
childhood grief?

20_____

20_____

20_____

August

25

What does forgiveness mean to you?

20____ _____

_____

_____

_____

_____

20____ _____

_____

_____

_____

_____

20____ _____

_____

_____

_____

_____

26

What does your partner do that makes you feel loved?

20_____

20_____

20_____

August

27

Who had the biggest impact on you while you were growing up?

20____

20____

20____

28

Have you found your calling? If so, what is it?

20____

20____

20____

August

29

What could you do today or tomorrow to bring smile
on your partner's face?

20_____ _____

_____

_____

_____

_____

20_____ _____

_____

_____

_____

_____

20_____ _____

_____

_____

_____

_____

30

If you knew that your life will end in one week,
would you change anything about the way you are
now living? Why?

20____

20____

20____

August

31

Words you want to share with others?

20____ _____

_____

_____

_____

20____ _____

_____

_____

_____

20____ _____

_____

_____

_____

1

How can you add more fun into everyday life?

20____

20____

20____

September

2

Write a gratitude letter to your past self

20____

20____

20____

3

How do you deal with emotional pain?

20____

20____

20____

September

4

How do you recharge, rejuvenate your energy?

20____

20____

20____

5

Words you like to say to a deceased loved one?

20____

20____

20____

September

6

What is your mind focused on recently and why?

20_____ _____

20_____ _____

20_____ _____

7

List some cultural beliefs you think are outdated

20____

20____

20____

September

8

List some favorite jokes

20_____

20_____

20_____

9

Your appreciation to your partner

20_____

20_____

20_____

September

10

Your view on fame, wealthy and happiness

20_____

20_____

20_____

11

How are you taking care of yourself?

20_____

20_____

20_____

September

12

A moment that challenged you

20_____

20_____

20_____

13

What is the purpose of relationship?

20____

20____

20____

September

14

If you had to go a week without your phone, what
would you miss the most about it?

20_____

20_____

20_____

15

Something that you like about your partner you
think they may not know?

20_____

20_____

20_____

September

16

If you could live anywhere for a year, where would you choose? why?

20_____

20_____

20_____

17

What questions have you been dying to ask ?

20_____

20_____

20_____

September

18

What is the inspiring book you have read?

20_____ _____

_____

_____

_____

_____

20_____ _____

_____

_____

_____

_____

20_____ _____

_____

_____

_____

_____

19

What does attachment or non-attachment mean to
you ?

20_____

20_____

20_____

September

20

If you die now, would you have any regrets?

20_____ _____

_____

_____

_____

_____

20_____ _____

_____

_____

_____

_____

20_____ _____

_____

_____

_____

_____

21

Something I want to start doing… or keep doing… ?

20____

_____

_____

_____

_____

20____

_____

_____

_____

_____

20____

_____

_____

_____

_____

September

22

What would you do if you have one million dollars?

20_____ _____
_____
_____
_____
_____

20_____ _____
_____
_____
_____
_____

20_____ _____
_____
_____
_____
_____

23

If you could trade lives with anyone for a day, who
would it be and why?

20_____

20_____

20_____

September

24

What are empowering beliefs that you like to have?

20_____

_____

20_____

_____

20_____

_____

25

Wisdom is...Compassion is ...Beauty is...

20_____

20_____

20_____

September

26

What do you feel about death?

20____

20____

20____

27

Make a list of things you do or like to do to relax
yourself

20_____ _____

_____

_____

_____

_____

20_____ _____

_____

_____

_____

_____

20_____ _____

_____

_____

_____

_____

September

28

Your childhood self is looking at you in the eyes,
what would you say…?

20____ _____

_____

_____

_____

_____

20____ _____

_____

_____

_____

_____

20____ _____

_____

_____

_____

_____

29

What recent challenges are your grateful for?

20_____

20_____

20_____

September

30

What have you learned about yourself lately?

20___ _____

_____

_____

_____

_____

20___ _____

_____

_____

_____

_____

20___ _____

_____

_____

_____

_____

1

What habit would you most like to break and what habit would you most like to star?

20_____

_____

20_____

_____

20_____

_____

October

2

If relationship was a mirror, what do you see yourself
in it?

20___ _____

_____

_____

_____

_____

20___ _____

_____

_____

_____

_____

20___ _____

_____

_____

_____

_____

3

What is your favorite movie, why?

20_____

20_____

20_____

October

4

If you could make one change in the world, what would it be?

20_____ _____

_____

_____

_____

_____

20_____ _____

_____

_____

_____

_____

20_____ _____

_____

_____

_____

_____

5

What is the most loving thing you have done to yourself?

20____

20____

20____

October

6

What things are you really good at?

20___ _____

20___ _____

20___ _____

7

What's the accomplishment you are most proud of?

20_____ _____

_____

_____

_____

20_____ _____

_____

_____

_____

20_____ _____

_____

_____

_____

October

8

What things done by your partner that you are grateful for?

20_____

20_____

20_____

9

Recent mistake that helped you to grow?

20____

20____

20____

October

10

Top 3 favorite memories together

20____ _____

_____

_____

_____

_____

20____ _____

_____

_____

_____

20____ _____

_____

_____

_____

_____

11

What beliefs are holding you back from being who you truly are?

20_____

20_____

20_____

October

12

The quality you admire the most in others is…why?

20_____

20_____

20_____

13

What blessings or/and miracles have you experienced?

20_____

20_____

20_____

October

14

What childish thing do you still enjoy?

20_____

20_____

20_____

15

If you designed and built a tree house, what would it
look like and what would be in it?

20____

20____

20____

October

16

What was the worst purchase you have ever made,
what did you learn about yourself?

20_____ _____

_____

_____

_____

_____

20_____ _____

_____

_____

_____

_____

20_____ _____

_____

_____

_____

_____

17

What do you believe even though you know it's probably wrong?

20____ _____

20____ _____

20____ _____

October

18

Where do you see yourself in two years?

20_____ _____

_____

_____

_____

_____

20_____ _____

_____

_____

_____

_____

20_____ _____

_____

_____

_____

_____

19

What was your proudest moment?

20_____

20_____

20_____

October

20

What is your favorite childhood memory?

20_____ _____

_____

_____

_____

_____

20_____ _____

_____

_____

_____

_____

20_____ _____

_____

_____

_____

_____

21

How would you spend your 100th birthday?

20____

_____

_____

_____

_____

20____

_____

_____

_____

_____

20____

_____

_____

_____

_____

October

22

What are the sweetest heartfelt things your partner
has ever said to you?

20____

_____

_____

_____

_____

20____

_____

_____

_____

_____

20____

_____

_____

_____

_____

23

What were your fear-based thoughts or actions?

20____

20____

20____

October

24

What were your love-based thoughts or actions?

20_____ _____

_____

_____

_____

_____

20_____ _____

_____

_____

_____

_____

20_____ _____

_____

_____

_____

_____

25

What would you like to do together with your
partner that you have never done before?

20_____

_____

_____

_____

_____

20_____

_____

_____

_____

_____

20_____

_____

_____

_____

_____

October

26

What triggers your emotion?

20____ _____

_____

_____

_____

20____ _____

_____

_____

_____

20____ _____

_____

_____

_____

October

27

What does your ideal day look like?

20____

20____

20____

October

28

Go back in time what would you tell your partner
how awesome your partner turn out?

20____ _____

_____

_____

_____

_____

20____ _____

_____

_____

_____

_____

20____ _____

_____

_____

_____

_____

29

A time you showed strength when you could have given up?

20____ _____

_____

_____

_____

_____

20____ _____

_____

_____

_____

_____

20____ _____

_____

_____

_____

_____

October

30

Times in your life you wish you would have had your partner with you?

20_____

_____

20_____

_____

20_____

_____

31

How do you deal with rejection?

20____

20____

20____

November

1

When is a time you were very proud to be together
with our partner?

20____ _____
_____
_____
_____
_____

20____ _____
_____
_____
_____
_____

20____ _____
_____
_____
_____
_____

2

What something you were really stressed about, it
turned out to be no big deal?

20_____

20_____

20_____

November

3

What events made the biggest impact on who you
are today?

20____ _____

_____

_____

_____

_____

20____ _____

_____

_____

_____

_____

20____ _____

_____

_____

_____

_____

4

What is something you have read or heard that has
stuck with you for a long time?

20____

20____

20____

November

5

What are the skills you like to learn?

20_____ _____

_____

_____

_____

_____

20_____ _____

_____

_____

_____

_____

20_____ _____

_____

_____

_____

_____

6

What's something you always wanted to do as a
child but never got to do?

20_____

20_____

20_____

November

7

What in your life do you feel grateful for?

20____ _____

_____

_____

_____

_____

20____ _____

_____

_____

_____

_____

20____ _____

_____

_____

_____

_____

8

What do you like to do on the weekend?

20_____

_____

20_____

_____

20_____

_____

November

9

What/who inspires you and why?

20_____

20_____

20_____

10

What is your definition of self-love, is it selfish or necessary, why do you hold this belief?

20____

20____

20____

November

11

Your observation on living in Cultural Matrix that shapes our values and beliefs?

20_____

_____

20_____

_____

20_____

_____

12

Write down things your mind has been whispering?

20_____ _____

_____

_____

_____

_____

20_____ _____

_____

_____

_____

_____

20_____ _____

_____

_____

_____

_____

November

13

What is your highest vision about yourself?

20_____

20_____

20_____

14

What's a belief that you hold with many people disagree?

20_____

20_____

20_____

November

15

Have you done anything recently worth
remembering?

20_____ _____

_____

_____

_____

_____

20_____ _____

_____

_____

_____

_____

20_____ _____

_____

_____

_____

_____

16

Are you holding onto something that you need to let go?

20_____

20_____

20_____

November

17

What do you respond when you don't get what you want?

20_____ _____

_____

_____

_____

_____

20_____ _____

_____

_____

_____

_____

20_____ _____

_____

_____

_____

_____

18

If you could relive one day of your life, what day
would it be and why?

20_____ _____

_____

_____

_____

_____

20_____ _____

_____

_____

_____

_____

20_____ _____

_____

_____

_____

_____

November

19

The little things I can enjoy right now are…

20_____ _____

20_____ _____

20_____ _____

20

I am thankful for my family experience because…

20____ _____

_____

_____

_____

_____

20____ _____

_____

_____

_____

_____

20____ _____

_____

_____

_____

_____

November

21

I am thankful for my ability to…

20____

20____

20____

22

What guidance or clarity you like to receive from the Universe?

20____

20____

20____

November

23

The most inspiring person you have ever met in person and why

20_____ _____

_____

_____

_____

_____

20_____ _____

_____

_____

_____

_____

20_____ _____

_____

_____

_____

24

A few words of advice about life to your children or
someone younger

20____

20____

20____

November

25

How do you feel about your communication skill and
what would you like to improve?

20_____ _____

_____

_____

_____

_____

20_____ _____

_____

_____

_____

_____

20_____ _____

_____

_____

_____

_____

26

How do you take your worry away?

20_____

20_____

20_____

November

27

One good/kind thing you can do tomorrow and why?

20____ _____

_____

_____

_____

_____

20____ _____

_____

_____

_____

_____

20____ _____

_____

_____

_____

_____

28

3 things you are proud of?

20____

20____

20____

November

29

How do you handle disagreements?

20_____ _____

20_____ _____

20_____ _____

30

How happy are you with the amount of time you spend together?

20_____

_____

20_____

_____

20_____

_____

December

1

How did you make each other smile this week?

20_____ _____

_____

_____

_____

20_____ _____

_____

_____

_____

20_____ _____

_____

_____

_____

2

If your love story were written, what would be the
title and why?

20____ _____

_____

_____

_____

20____ _____

_____

_____

_____

20____ _____

_____

_____

_____

December

3

What do you believe to be your gifts/talents?

20____ _____

_____

_____

_____

_____

20____ _____

_____

_____

_____

_____

20____ _____

_____

_____

_____

_____

4

Events you are looking forward to?

20____

20____

20____

December

5

What do you believe you deserve in life?

20____ _____

_____

_____

_____

_____

_____

20____ _____

_____

_____

_____

_____

_____

20____ _____

_____

_____

_____

_____

_____

6

What does healthy relationship mean and provide
for the people in it?

20_____

_____

20_____

_____

20_____

_____

December

7

Do you usually follow your head or your heart when making decision?

20____

20____

20____

8

What's the best way to end a long day?

20____ _____

_____

_____

_____

20____ _____

_____

_____

_____

_____

20____ _____

_____

_____

_____

_____

December

9

Have you shifted perspectives? What and why?

20____ _____

20____ _____

20____ _____

10

What music do you listen that lighten up your energy?

20____

20____

20____

December

11

What documentary you enjoy or inspires you?

20____ _____

_____

_____

_____

_____

20____ _____

_____

_____

_____

_____

20____ _____

_____

_____

_____

_____

12

Every day do something you enjoy. What would you do in the next 3 days?

20____

20____

20____

December

13

What does the new year mean to you?

20_____ _____

_____

_____

_____

_____

20_____ _____

_____

_____

_____

_____

20_____ _____

_____

_____

_____

_____

14

What would you like to create next year?

20____

20____

20____

December

15

What would you like to learn from scratch?

20_____ _____

_____

_____

_____

20_____ _____

_____

_____

_____

20_____ _____

_____

_____

_____

16

What's your favorite memory with your partner this year?

20___

_____

20___

_____

20___

_____

December

17

What does Christmas mean to you?

20_____

20_____

20_____

18

Appreciation to your children or someone younger
in the family

20＿＿＿

20＿＿＿

20＿＿＿

December

19

How mindful are you?

20_____

20_____

20_____

20

If you can make someone smile, who would it be and why?

20_____

20_____

20_____

December

21

What does your inner wisdom tell you to have love
and peace today?

20____ _____

_____

_____

_____

_____

20____ _____

_____

_____

_____

_____

20____ _____

_____

_____

_____

_____

22

List 3 positive relationship acts for love marriage or family bond?

20_____

_____

_____

_____

_____

20_____

_____

_____

_____

_____

20_____

_____

_____

_____

_____

December

23

Who would you like to connect (or reconnect) with, why?

20_____

20_____

20_____

24

How do you nourish yourself physically, emotionally
and spiritually?

20_____

_____

_____

_____

_____

20_____

_____

_____

_____

_____

20_____

_____

_____

_____

_____

December

25

Christmas gifts you sent and received?

20____

_____

20____

_____

20____

_____

26

Experiences you look forward to have?

20_____

20_____

20_____

December

27

List appreciation to yourself this year?

20_____ _____

_____

_____

_____

20_____ _____

_____

_____

_____

20_____ _____

_____

_____

_____

28

List appreciation to your partner this year?

20____ _____

_____

_____

_____

_____

20____ _____

_____

_____

_____

_____

20____ _____

_____

_____

_____

_____

December

29

List appreciation to your family/friend this year?

20_____ _____

_____

_____

_____

_____

20_____ _____

_____

_____

_____

_____

20_____ _____

_____

_____

_____

_____

30

What good you received this year in the form of love,
hope, faith, inspiration or in many other ways?

20_____

20_____

20_____

December

31

Give thanks and appreciation. I am grateful for…

20_____

20_____

20_____

Made in the USA
Las Vegas, NV
26 January 2023

66307489R00203